More

More

Poems

Arlene Weiner

RAGGED SKY PRESS
PRINCETON, NEW JERSEY

Published by Ragged Sky Press
270 Griggs Drive, Princeton, NJ 08540
www.raggedsky.com

Library of Congress Control Number: 2022943241
ISBN: 978-1-933974-50-7
Cover and book design: Dirk Rowntree
Photograph of author: Ellen Foos
Printed in the United States of America
First Edition

I like the trivial, vulgar, and exalted.

—*J. V. Cunningham*

Contents

I

Curriculum Vitae

Frenchy Cannoli, Ardent Evangelist for Hashish,
Dies at 64. —N.Y. Times, *July 31, 2021.*

The little round of life.
The unicycle on the tightrope,
the yellow parasol. The Monday wash,
the Wednesday fold.

While Frenchy Cannoli lived in a cave
in the Parvati Valley
studying traditional methods
of making hashish from resin

I was toiling in the penetralia
of the rare book room at Harvard
hoping to add a fresh crumb
to the hill of received knowledge.

I was not marrying three times,
divorcing once, becoming once widowed,
not hanging at CBGB or scuffing my shoes
on the cobbles in the Left Bank.

I was not riding pillion on a cycle
nor trekking in Katmandu.
I birthed two sons,
was a den mother, a school volunteer.

Some evenings I took our laundry
to Norge Village, entered it into
a gleaming bank of washers and dryers.
My dissertation was published and forgotten.

I built a compost heap, moved,
built another. Frenchy Cannoli,
scholar of hash, has died—he too
has begun to improve the soil.

Kalte Milch

Love chased me with a cup
of milk *with the chill taken off.*
American child, I liked milk cold.

Old fear drew Love to me always,
to follow, feed, fill. Love pinched
my fat cheeks, my thighs, needed
to know I wouldn't disappear,
grow ill, turn chill as winter earth.

Love had already lost so many
to cold, fever, dearth.

These Days

As girls we trained for these days:
keeping our distance, indoor languor,
waiting in patience—
bespoke garments on a hanger
waiting to be worn. Thorns vined
around our cool limbs.

Alone before bed
we brushed our hair
one hundred times. We shone
through windows, behind
veils. Skirts trammeled us, corsets
constrained our breath.

The castle sleeps. Now
granddaughters and grandsons
await the kiss of a vaccine
to wake them to life,
to busyness, release them
from these days.

Wordless

My mother's magazines advised
"togetherness," advertised Simplicity patterns

for matching mother-and-daughter dresses,
asked "Can This Marriage Survive?"

I found *Popular Science,* admired
the clear lines and cheerful mien

of "Wordless Workshop." Each month
a pointy-nosed hero, handy husband,

briefly studied some problem: scattered
towels, shattered glass. Not long perplexed,

he set to work next with dowels and drill,
assembled some device shown in panel 2

overhead, in exploded view. Oh daddy!

The men came home from Korea,
the Rosenbergs were executed, the H-bomb

flowered over the Pacific. We schoolchildren
were issued dog tags. Gary McMann told me

*When you hear sirens put your tag in your mouth
in case your head is blown off.*

Twelve drawings in the Wordless Workshop.
In the last one, the wife, the child, the dog are happy.

Europe

A postcard from my mother's aunt
to her sister: *Dorothy,*
why didn't you come with us?
Aboard the Bremen. 1930.

On the other side, a picture of her,
smiling, fashionable,
in the Piazza San Marco,
pigeon wings all around her.

She was a rich relation, generous
to my widowed grandmother
and her five children. She would come
to their place in Brooklyn
to give my mother, the youngest,
a ride in her Duesenberg.

Maybe she took Grandma
for an abortion
when my grandfather died at 32
of a pulmonary clot.

My mother grew up treasuring gifts
she brought back from her trips:
hand-embroidered handkerchiefs,
a music box from Switzerland.

In the 1960s, when my mother and father
had enough money,
finally, to travel a little,
my mother wanted to go to Europe.

My father, born in Poland, said, *To me,*
Europe is a cemetery.

Yizkor (Remembrance Service)

No one alive can remember
the woman I will call Bluma.
I'm saying Kaddish—it's not called for,
she was no relation to me—for Bluma.
The Kaddish exalts the Name. She is nameless,
so I give her a name, lift her up.

In Jezierzany, the town my father left at ten,
she was a *kurveh*—a whore—
whether for pay or for pleasure
I don't know. She'd send her simple son
to pick up the red wrapping papers
of chicory to rub on her cheeks.

Whores deserve life.
Simpletons deserve life.
She did what she needed to do.
In a fairytale a *shochet*—a kosher butcher—
might have fallen for her red cheeks,
married her, taken her to Canada or Australia.

In 1920 my father left that town,
that country, that continent.
If Bluma hadn't died before,
if her simple son had survived,
if they remained in Jezierzany,
they died in spring, 1943
with one thousand two hundred others.

What You're Proudest of Is Not What Your Grandchildren Will Admire You For

You may have devoted years
to discovering the Higgs boson
but what impresses them is
taking them to lunch with a Groucho nose on.

You've photographed birds
from Amazonia to Antarctica on life-list hunts
but they boast to their playmates that they saw you
pick up an earthworm barehanded once.

They plug up their ears at your lectures
even if your TED Talk went viral
but are astonished when you pare an apple
in one continuous spiral.

Maybe you've led demonstrations
against intercontinental missiles?
They'd rather you demonstrate
how you produce call-me-a-taxi whistles.

Accomplishments lauded
and awarded by your peers
are eclipsed by children's applause
when you juggle or wiggle your ears.

But all the above
is lagniappe,
what's really important is love,
and a comfortable lap.

Lament for Cursive

Time does not flow.—Carlo Rovelli

My mother looks up, sees
atop her closet in the nursing home
a photograph of my brother and me
that she tinted by hand. *Look at the pictures,*
when I see them I'm happy.

Starlight is coming toward us
from extinct stars. In those days
we dressed for photographs,
a special occasion, so my hair's tight-permed,
soon to relax into its usual straightness.

We all have plans for a tree house
in a tree that fell on the wires
next door. We all carry keys
to a house that burned down.
Look at the pictures. Look.

Draw a Clock

I left a message, Mom, are you okay?
She recently said, I have trouble with numbers.
She didn't return my call yesterday.

When she tries to dial, she fumbles,
so she didn't return my call
when I left a message, Mom, are you okay?

She was a bookkeeper, then worked
for the phone company. Always numbers.
She didn't return my call yesterday.

She recently said, I was so good
with numbers. Now I can't remember.
I left a message, Mom, are you okay?

yesterday and the day before.
Last time I visited she said
I can't do numbers any more.

On the Draw a Clock test
she put the numbers all on one side.
She said, I can't do numbers,
held up her fingers. I can do five.

For My Mother

Adele Weitz, 1916–2020

How can I get my arms around you?
How can I see you clearly when you were my light?
How can I embrace you when you were my sky?
My first feeder, my first teacher.

If I love trees, it's because they are like your legs when I was small.
If I love words, it's because they are like your murmurs over my crib.
If I love poetry, it's because you were consoled by a poem.
If I love the world, it's because you taught me to love.

I won't look for you in the stars—
Your constellation shines on earth.

Paper Boats

Son, the secret fingers of my body
folded your body like the paper boats
in the Tagore poem my mother read me.
He wished his boats to carry messages
to those downstream.

When you blew soap bubbles
in the mountains, I said
you were sending them
to children in the valley.

My mother folded her life into me,
looked to unfold me and read her story,
but you are not my letter to the world—
steer yourself in the world's fast current.

More

The plastic bag promises *12 Grain Bread,*
and I laugh. If one grain is good, should twelve
be better? *Are* there twelve good grains?
And I remember, it's Shavuot,
the Feast of Weeks, a festival
I don't completely understand, the end
of the seven times seven days' count
of the omer—something to do with grain.
Wheat, I assume, the staff of life.
I'm shopping for my son's little family,
whole grain for my grandson.

I look at the label to count the grains:
Whole wheat flour (one), *malted barley flour* (two),
rye, oats, (four), *corn grits, sunflower seeds*

(not a grain, but be generous, say six),
brown rice (seven), *triticale* (eight),
barley, buckwheat (a grass; let it pass—
ten), *flaxseed* (don't know), *millet* (twelve),
soy grits. A baker's dozen?
Most of them listed after *molasses.*

Before he could speak my grandson learned
two ASL signs, *Finished, More,*
like the first wordless words
at the breast, turning away
or latching on.

More grains, more good,
more goods, the large life.

The festival of Shavuot celebrates first fruits,
seven kinds, and the early harvest of barley, not wheat.
(I've looked it up now.) The rabbis say
the forty-nine days of counting the omer

restrain the excitement of receiving the Torah
at Sinai. After forty years in the desert
endured by twelve tribes.

My grandson has speech now.
I sing for him,

Do you know the muffin man,
his favorite song,
hardly finish before he says, *More!*

II

Second Acts

The factory's about to close.
Your birth mother shows up
needing a kidney. War is declared.
You'll have to sell your goat.
The principal suspect turns up dead.
You were switched at birth
for Frances Gumm. After
a youth of eating vegan cheese
you discover butter. You've been
living a lie. He's been living a lie.
They've been living a lie.
Living's a lie. At the window,
a white face that looks familiar.

Mantis

Far from any tree or blade of grass
on a street where sparrows
chirped above a storefront
it appeared in my bedroom

We children believed there was
a two-hundred-dollar fine
for killing a mantis
but who would have hurt it

so green and large and human
so upright and grasping
surely an ambassador
to me in that room

where my mother drew down
the dark green shade
that in summer admitted
pinpoints of light

my first constellations

On the Land

I pulled some plants that showed too-early green
when I might have been writing poetry.
On the way to the compost heap
with a kind of bouquet—fleshy roots, round leaves—
I thought of a poet-farmer-prophet
who urges *Get back to your roots.*
Back to the land. To soil and toil,
to your home place, your forefathers' place.

My roots are in Manhattan, north
of Harlem. When my sixth-grade teacher
gave us morning-glory seeds
I dug dirt from the park to plant mine, guiltily.
A white worm arched out. I shuddered
and buried it. Buried it again, until
it unfolded green wings. Oh poet,
my forefathers had no land,
but now in my garden in Pittsburgh
wrens build, rabbits browse, and rhododendron
open waterlily blooms to bees in June.

After the Emergence of the Periodical Cicadas

Under an oak near the high school in June
like pompoms discarded after a game,
a circle of stemmed and rustling clusters—
bouquets of cicada brides whose courtship
made the sky sing so in May.
The wedding music stopped, these are left,
to be caught by maidens in seventeen years.

Love that waits seventeen years,
buried love that sounds in our ears
as present as silence, hopeful love,
that scatters its sons and daughters
on the charity of the world—how can we not
side with it, shelter it, or stand aside
as it casts into the future
as if there were peace in nature.

Love-Apple

Blood-bead berry,
like the purple-flowered
weed that creeps in the garden,
when I brush against your leaves
you leave your particular scent.

No hornworm come
between us, nightshade,
no blight spoil your bloom,
your Edenic fruit.

I protect you, fence you,
watch against predators
until blushing, dusky,
you please my eyes,
fall ready into my hand.

Smooth skin resisting,
burst in my mouth,
answer crush with tang,
surprise my tongue
with juice, my first,
my little one.

November

Not because I'm beautiful, but because
I was the only one out this morning,
rooting out standing weeds,
raking red and yellow leaves,
"putting the garden to bed,"
the old man rubbed his raspy cheek
against mine, kissed my fingertips.

He is no curly-haired boy
who drops to one knee
to ask me to dance.
He tears off summer's dress,
exposes trunk and limb, threatens
worse coming. Yet he brings gifts:
Red birds among the berries, clear nights,
Orion's diamond stars, ermine streets.

Doves

First snowflakes. I count
gray doves in the crabapple.
My wealth.

Wildlings

The neighbors' back stairs rotted away.
Once a year, they hired someone
to push a heavy mower round their yard.

At the edges, a rank succession
of ragged interlopers encroached.
I'd sneak in to pull weeds I didn't like.

The sunlit circle shrank, darkened,
like a house with closed-off rooms.
Grass gave way to weeds,

weeds gave way to bushes,
small trees found purchase,
overwintered.

I have little wildness in me
but I don't clean the corners of my field
where creatures glean and hide at need.

I cultivate the accidentals,
the volunteers, some of them natives,
let bee-balm, goldenrod, asters set seed,

invite cardinal, finch, bee,
squirrel, chipmunk,
rabbit, butterfly, robin,

and I hope the sea-eagle
that escaped its local "habitat"—
a cage?— stays free, stays wild.

On a Park Bench with Richard St. John

We watch children pass, the young,
beginning to be men and women.

I am not young.
And the children I carried in my belly,
the children I expelled from my body
when the doctor held up the velvet placenta
and declared them male
are not young.

Forgiveness is a cup of water.

A child breaks a branch off a park tree
casually, irreparably,
and the mother and father
continue, maybe praising
the child's growing strength.

Do you offer the cup of water?

Do you give water to strangers
and to enemies, drinkers of blood,
from a never-drying source?

Who carries the water?

With dry throat
I mourn the broken branch,
the velvet bud.

For a Friend with Ashes on Her Forehead

In Lent you sacrifice
and we Jews in Passover,
holding our breath for spring,
as if an absent father
returns, hands held behind him,
smiles and says, *Which hand?*
and the expected surprise
comes if we are good,
not if God is good.
Sometimes God shows
both hands empty, or full of nails.

In my generation many children
were burnt to ash.
One Jewish boy in a photograph,
at gunpoint, hands raised,
survived, grew old. Grown,
should he sacrifice bread and meat?

Why bind the thigh with barbs,
why blink away beauty?
Why is the world not enough?
Why not rejoice in the muscular
and circular motions of nature
though weevils breed in the grain,
bread greens in the cupboard?

I won't blame the drownings
on the carnival, the carnage
on drunkenness.
Hope: a sweet taste, not nutriment.
Resurrection: the skully grin
of Jack-in-the-box put back,
the spring of our own stored hope.
Our ratcheted plucky music calls him forth.

Pluck up that music for dancing,
let the thighs' corduroy friction
recall simplicity, break bread
not bones, join healed empty hands,
pour wine and call the stranger to the feast.
If God be thanked, thank God for appetite.

Law

Who shall avenge unreason? —J.V. Cunningham

Gusts heave the trees in full leaf
like green seas. Some that are bare
are spared the violent thrust.

Near streams, trees lean for a share
of sun. Then after soaking rains
some fall, become bridges, dams.

Yesterday I heard jays scream,
searched for their trouble, saw
a hawk on a thick limb, holding prey down.

No fault in those that put out leaves
like sails in the wind, that lean to light,
that build and breed under the sky.

Kathleen's dying now at home, who earned
better, if good deeds, good spirit earn good.
No prudence could avert this death,
no reward recompense.

Because We Are Not Angels

Why not thank God for gravity
in which we move and have our being
as fish swim, drink, and taste the sea
their fins like prayer flags fluttering?

Why wish for flight? Each step a fall
forward, we trust as gannets trust
the air, launching from bluffs,
relying on our mothering planet's pull
each one-foot-in-front-of-the-other day.

And why not wonder at number and all
the natural laws? Being fallen, we pause
to feel the heart's chambers pulse
only when its meter fibrillates, fails.

III

Smallwares

My mother didn't teach me
to sew. I never mastered
the rhythmically galloping treadle,
the thrust thrust thrust of the needle
as her left hand pushed cloth,
right hand turned a wheel.
She feared I'd be hurt.

When I was pregnant, I bought
a portable electric machine
to sew for my baby,
edged squares of flannel
for receiving blankets
and washcloths,
but I didn't continue to sew.

Today I stitched up the sleeve
of my husband's knit jacket, ineptly.
I thought of the lost arts: darning,
reweaving, making and mending.
I thought of women's smallwares:
pinking shears, thimbles, darning eggs,
seam rippers, knitting needles, crochet hooks.

The second time I gave birth
my labor slowed down, and the doctor
approached with a big crochet hook
to break my bag of waters.
The Supreme Court is considering
whether a woman should be permitted
to end a pregnancy. That hook
looked like a clothes hanger,
which some women have used.

Women used to be more able,
at sewing and having babies,
than I have been.

I'm thinking about ripping seams,
stitching and unstitching,
keeping on or giving up.

Tree of Life

I marked myself *safe* on Facebook
when the alert came: active shooter
in my neighborhood.
Is *safe* a lie if you want to believe it?

I never feel safe.
When I was eight my playmate Patsy
came home from her school
and asked me *Why did you kill Christ?*
I had no answer.

Ambushed by strangers
near the synagogue,
I spilled my Hebrew-school books,
their top-heavy black letters.

At Hallowe'en I defended
my kid brother, socked with nylons
full of powdered chalk,
his jacket marked, unsafe.

I saw a movie of bulldozers
burying skeletal dead.

Shelter in place, the notice said.
My friends and neighbors text,
and I tell you: *Stay safe.*

Security Training—Stop the Bleed

*—The US Department of Homeland Security
advises remembering: "Run, Hide, Fight."*

Run. Escape if you can.
Walk across Russia to Austria.
Get on a train to Rotterdam.
Emigrate to Cuba, which has an unfilled quota.

Hide. Shelter in place.
Shave your beard, bleach your hair.
Get a nose job.
Change your name.

Fight. As a last resort.
Look around you—everyday objects
can become weapons. Hot coffee. Pencils.
Throw accurately and with force. Strike
without apology.

Run. Hide. Fight.
Never again. Again. Again.

This Poem Is a Stone

A small hard thing.
It says, I stood here.
This stone is made of tears.
A heavy thing.
These tears say peace upon you.
A hard, heavy thing.

Even a stone
does not last forever.
This hard, heavy thing
will not last forever
but it will last
a long, long time.

Resistance

Make friends with policemen and soldiers.
Read them the Nuremberg Laws.
Memorize poetry. Catch rainwater.
Take in stray animals. You may have to eat them.
Meanwhile, they'll warm you.

Seventy years old, the Old Believer
lives in the taiga like the last Japanese soldier
in a cave, who kept sharpened sticks
to repel the invasion
he was certain would come.

Near Jerzyiany, my father's town,
two families lived
in an underground cavern
for twenty months, sent a son
to barter for potatoes.

Could I live without light? Could I kill?

September, 2017

As fire ants cling, self-rafting,
resist the punishing flood, form
one body. *But meeting black ants, red
will conquer, devour.*

Yesterday for an hour
I heard Shakespeare trumpet
war's costs—orphans, men dismembered,
daughters defiled—yet heard
wild verse drum on to slaughter.

In new wars, no bannered colors,
stirring pipes. North against South
won't throw man against man. No
demilitarized zone. Only the nose cone,
isolate silo, eye of drone.

Dead Russian Soldier

Stretched out in a foreign city
claimed to be his country's.
How old? Eighteen, twenty?
Patriotism or mere obedience
brought him here.
Should we hate him, or pity?
We in the West aren't clear
of blood and expedient
excuse for conquest.

Mother of this soldier, my hand
to you. My father lived in the land
where your son lies unburied,
now wasted by fire once again,
my kin were slaughtered there,
interred unhonored. I hear
Slava Ukraini! Words of glory—
this bloody story never ends.

Bombs

When gay men threw particles of glitter
like disco fairy dust at politicians
who opposed same-sex marriage
they were *glitter-bombing*.

In the *New York Times*
a psychologist warns about *love-bombing,*
a preface to malevolent control.
In recent slang *da bomb* meant *great*.

You can *photobomb, zoombomb,*
but aren't those forms of bombing different
from what bombing actually is? Sudden, yes,
unwelcome, yes, even damaging, maybe.

A *New Yorker* cover from the 1940s shows
a sleeping boy, smiling as he dreams
of a fighter plane shooting down German aircraft.
Puffs of smoke, death spirals. Because *bomb*
to one meant *balm* to others.

A man I know watched a World War II movie
as a boy, excited, rooting for the bombers.
His German-American mother said
Everyone cries for his own kind.

The plane is a fighter, not a bomber, the boy
dreams of being a champion, single, brave,
maybe protecting bigger, slow, bombers,
that could kill wholesale. There's that word, *kill*—

we slid over *death* in *death spiral,* which now
has been tamed to metaphor. We slide
over the harms we do to others, excited,
until we cry for our own kind.

Dear Editor:

We've subscribed to your magazine
for a long time. We remember
your recommendations for canned tomatoes
and comparison of the nutritive value
of brands of store bread, when those
were a good chunk of our budget.
We'd never think of buying
a refrigerator or a car
without consulting your ratings.

But I want to suggest that you run a question
alongside every product listing
like the chyron of a newscast:
Do you really need this? Do you *need*
a gasoline-powered leaf blower,
a riding mower? Maybe if you used
a manual mower and a leaf rake
you wouldn't need a Peloton.

Do you need a hundred-thirty-dollar yoga mat?
I'm pretty sure the Seven Sages didn't schlep
a cushy mat with them on their travels.
Do you need a portable backyard pizza oven?
If you used it indoors, you might die
of carbon monoxide poisoning.

Dear Editor, we might all die
of carbon dioxide poisoning
the atmosphere, a smothering blanket. All:
the elephants, the whales, the corals, the redwoods,
our grandmothers, grandchildren, selves: burnt
in a fire in California, drowned
in a basement in New York City, starved
on a desiccated Hopi reservation, fallen
from a raft packed with refugees
from desertification, abandoned

on an exhausting journey from a hopeless place
where the land no longer sustains a population.

I admit my household has enough, and even too much,
and so I speak from a position of privilege.
Editor, I think you have good intentions and do good.
I just want to remind you: Consumption,
a wasting disease, is fatal.

The All-American Truck Stop

In Carlisle, Pennsylvania, was our habitual stop
between the place where we were raising our kids
and where we were raised. Half-way.
In the section reserved for truckers, phones
at every table. We ate in the regular section.
Sometimes, it's true, we stopped at the Big Boy
with its smiling effigy of the Boy, as big
as our own two boys, holding up a platter of burgers,
but the All-American was our go-to place.

Flag-waving was common then, time
of Love It or Leave It—before then
the flag flew in a foreign country,
or on the moon, a declaration,
Here an American stands, or stood,
but then flag-waving passed into jingoism,
signing hostility to those
who opposed hostilities in Vietnam.

It took quite a while before I noticed
the etchings in glass of the football hero,
the clippings about Jim Thorpe,
who'd gone to—or been kidnapped to—
the Carlisle Indian School, and I realized
the All-American Truck Stop
was named for Jim Thorpe, All-American.

Honor to Jim Thorpe, honor to those
who honored him. The All-American Truck Stop
has passed, and the Big Boy, too,
the Chinese restaurant, the tattoo parlor.
Our boys are men now, tall.
The truck stop's a franchise. Last time
I drove through, even the building
that held the Army War College
was vacant, up for sale.

IV

How Not to Look Old

Throned on a scooter
Anita steered imperially
through wide aisles

Now breathless she sleeps away
the bright afternoon
while I leaf through a magazine

whose name
O
holds a hoop high for women
younger than we

The cover of *O* teases *How
Not to Look Old*
Inside the first ten ways
not to look old
have to do with hair

O
how like hole,
how like halo
zero

We who have holes
or are holes
we
who in the world
had no shadow
deemed shadows
of men

At the checkout I paid
The cashier whispered
Is she your mom?

How not to look old

Die young
Die fast
Not the slow drip way of chemo
Not pregnant everywhere
with tyrannous ovary

I lift my eyes
to a west-facing window
to watch that dangerous O the sun

That big bright O visibly sinks
between tall oaks

No
it is fixed
we turn away from it
into the night
where all are shadowless

Once Again Facebook Suggests That I Friend Someone I Know to Be Dead

Simplify, simplify, said Thoreau. The yard
needs pruning. The city charges now to take
yard waste, so branches and twigs already
fill three cans and threaten to block the alley.

The malady of too-muchness.
I've amassed so many books
that I'll never live long enough to read half
and indeed many are half read.

And if I friend the dead, will they be good friends?
Will they ask for recommendations,
start Go Fund Me appeals, tell me
they're traveling, need a paid-up debit card?

Facebook reminds me of Don's birthday,
Dorothy's. I think Facebook
is sorry for the dead, feels
they need more friends, more activity.

Patroclus begged Achilles
to give him funeral rites,
so he could join the other shades,
who held him at a distance.

Sometimes I post to Don
to tell him opera news or of a new
adaptation of *Gatsby.* Don, I remember
your white teeth, your California smile,

the Rhode Island beach we went to,
a long drive from Cambridge,
because there the sun sets over the sea,
as, you said, it's meant to.

Another Art

The art of losing isn't hard to master
—Elizabeth Bishop

The art of tossing is another thing.
I'm trying, really trying, to get clear.
So many objects seem to want to cling:

this antique toy that has a little ding,
the Pinewood Derby trophy—both so dear,
the art of tossing is another thing.

Put it on eBay, ka-ching, ka-ching—
keep nothing but the things that give you cheer.
But so many objects seem to want to cling

I'm very much afraid I'm weakening.
It's Fear of Missing Out, yes, fear
makes art of tossing yet another thing.

Here are some unread books—how can I fling
them out? Here, wedding gifts adhere
so! Many objects seem to want to cling.

At least I don't save ticket stubs or string!
I'll just look at these photos, have a beer—
and as for tossing—not another thing!
Too many objects seem to want to cling.

Serenade

In the morning in the bleached desert,
we sought blue shade, found footprints
of night mice in crevices where stone
crumbled into sand and sand compacted
to stone, where Joshua trees, aureoled in spines,
lifted few limbs toward the light.

One afternoon we lay weightless, face down
above corals, in water warm as a loved body,
nuzzled by fish, disc-shaped, snake-shaped,
striped, stippled, none bristling or venomous,
none startled or secretive.

Now under a sky winter-white, scrawled on
by bare branches, we look out on snow.
I remember young days eating dry seeds,
middle times of moist fruits, easy movement.
Night. I find you warm beside me, limbs still strong.

The Longest Night

December 21, 2013—for Ernie and Nancy

Most of our first year we grew in the dark
until, pitched into light, we drew harsh breath.
If evening brings us rest, that's our good luck.

Our mothers kept us safe from daily shock
warm in their lightless seas. Until our birth
most of our first year we grew in the dark.

Why should I fear the night, that means no work?
The crèche under the tree, the front door wreath
say, "Evening brings you rest." That's our good luck.

Lie down, loved dog. Don't wake her with a bark.
Tomorrow though light fails we'll venture forth.
Most of this year we've grown into the dark.

I'll lie down, too. Sleep with us—she may wake
for one last day. Dark, cover me like half the earth!
If evening brings me rest that's my good luck.

If I could find a star to pierce the murk....
She cools—give her your warmth. Your breath.
Most of this year we've grown dark, dark, dark.
If evening brings us rest, that's our good luck.

Pinky

Last week I took a shovel from a prepared heap,
scooped earth easily, turned, threw it
onto your coffin, plain pine.

Now I lean hard on a spade,
press into a hill of my making, good tilth.
I spread it, seed grass. I sweat.

I move earth as if to make the whole world even.
This is my yard. I'm intimate
with the dirt here, the worms,

can tell by the sound what resists:
the blade strikes thin plates of slate,
hard mill waste, tough roots, coal,

signs of who came before—
Indian head penny, tiny car,
water-green marble.

At ninety-five you were so small
I could have carried you alone,
laid you down,
lowered your body into the grave.

For the Widow at a Shiva

Dear frail friend, you were always delicate
but now the sun of death shines through you
as through our fingers those summer days
when the blue sky moved above us in illusory swarm
and we looked to the seventh wave.

You wear a torn ribbon, don't sit on the ground.
Someone explains that today is the 36th day
to count the omer, a ritual strange to us as a barley sheaf.
We have not studied this. I have not studied enough
to be your friend. Sorrow laps at us, recedes,
leaves a wrack we skirt for shining and ruined things.

In the Night

Someone is sitting beside you reciting.
The room must be cold, to hold you
from Friday to Sunday. All night
someone is near you, reading psalms,
as your mother read to you in your bed.
You do not hear. Outside this morning
I heard a bird say *keep, keep, keep,*
but we cannot keep you, cannot hold you.
You are still but you do not sleep.

For Loneliness

*—The Prime Minister of the U.K. has appointed a
Minister for Loneliness*

I know a woman who in widowhood
became enamored of a pet fish,
and a woman, long divorced,
who delights in seven fish,
each in his bowl.

During a time when I lived alone
I would hear a cricket chirping at night.
It fell silent as I passed through the room,
so I knew it knew me. And I grieved
when it no longer sang.

Minister for Loneliness, we have to sing
the angels back, we have to cherish
the creatures, even the smallest,
whose wings make song,
who may be the angels themselves.

Or by Lightning on the Golf Course

Raking the first leaves,
big brown pieces of torn-open wrapping,
I wish the oak would drop
all its leaves at once, get it over with,

grumpy because my ankle hurts from a fall
and I think there's permanent damage.
Last month my friend drew
in the air a diagram of decline:

something (say, cancer) happens
(a vertical drop)
you recover (he drew a plateau)
but you don't get back to the status quo—

next time another drop, another level,
and his finger described steps descending to…
that package still partly wrapped, the empty box.
Years of hurt. When to let go.

Some trees drop acorns,
rain buckeyes, leaves, branches,
shed bark, show fungus at the toe,
die back from the top.

Some go over intact,
root-ball in the air,
corona who knows where—
bring down wires, crash on a roof.

Steps like the ones in Carpentras
under the old synagogue,
descending into water.
Water so still I almost stepped in.

Breaking

That bridge I wrote about, a metaphor for connection,
  I called an "emblem of man's ambition,"
    so high above Fern Hollow, an "iron rainbow."

Some people feel they're in the hollow
  of God's hand, others always fear the anvil
    falling from an upstairs window,
      stray bullet, slippery sidewalk, tornado.

But this—it would take a virtuoso
  of worry to have imagined in the ordinary way
    of jogging, dogwalking, everyday commute,

That this steel ligature that bound two towns
  would snap.

When a volcano
  exploded in the sea off Tonga,
    the shock traveled around the world,

And the people of Tonga knew what to do:
  They ran for high ground, climbed trees,
    and one survived for nearly two days in the seas.

When an earthquake split Anchorage,
  a woman named Chance
    took to the airwaves for thirty hours,
      told people who needed help and where.

Here too, when our bridge collapsed
  there were people with savoir-faire,
    the man who scrambled up the ravine
      from his totaled car to tell others to halt;

The first responders who were lowered by rope
  and handed the stranded passengers up;

the ones who turned off the ruptured gas line;
   the woman leaving with the family go bag.

In extremis people astound
  with their presence of mind,
   extend hands to others, search the rubble.

Afterward, the trouble comes. Either you feel blessed,
  conscious, with every step, breath, or you never again
   trust the bridge, the sea, the ground.

V

Immersive Van Gogh

They'll be outdated soon, these widely advertised
commercial experiences: Projected on actual walls
when you could wear a VR headset to get all
the vertigo of orange, indigo, yellow.
One has a Spotify soundtrack,
splashes magnified petals on floors and ceilings too.

It's an ideal first date, dark, distanced:
Plunged into the hearts of giant sunflowers,
hold hands and imagine yourselves as bees.
One ad shows people as silhouettes
against deep blue and swirly white: *Starry Night!*
Not like the paintings I remember. No steeple, no trees.

I don't even like the gift-shop mug
that wraps Monet's haystacks around a cylinder,
warps what the artist painted flat.
But I'm being too hard on this art-adjacent
exhibit. Maybe immersing in his light and dark
will take us into van Gogh's own senses, disorient
us until, on the plain plank floor that rushes like a river,
the bed arrives, an orange boat we can mount
to sail into welcome comfort, a great ark.

Archery

For gym in college I elected archery.
We practiced in skirts on the tiny sward
in the center of our urban campus.
Once Bob Pack, my writing teacher, passed,
caught my eye, pointed at his heart.

I remember Joan Brown, a Diana,
putting shot after shot into the gold.
Eye, bow hand steady, fletching
between the fingers, tension, draw,
release, palm grazing cheek, ear,
the arrow trembling in the target.

Surely the bow came before the lyre—
some playful hunter plucked
the useful string.

By the Neva River, where I have never been

I am unfolding a newspaper under the trees.
It's autumn, ripened fruits overhead,
when I look up and see a young-old man cruise by—
it's Federico Garcia Lorca, no longer dead!

Hey, poet, sit down for a minute, though I'm straight
and you're sixty years older, at least.
I'd like to light your silver-tipped black cigarette,
and buy blinis with sour cream to break your fast.

What are you doing here? It's the Days of Awe.
I stole a few good lines from you—that *branched thigh,*
the *sleeping water*—so I must ask forgiveness, by Jewish law.
And what am I doing in Leningrad, by the by,
an unreadable Cyrillic paper in my paw?

Does it encrypt who shall live, who shall die?

Square Poems Don't Satisfy Carlos
—for C.H.P.

he coaxes me to   open up
puts spaces in places   I haven't thought of,
slashes and splashes   across the page
like tracks on the towpath
                after rain

        he's tactful about spare
        wear-with-anything poems
        like safe dark dresses

Ay Carlos, can I truly
grind grist on a hot stone
add lard and lye, pat a poem round
fill it with milk and meat?

        not offer only crisp lines, ruly
        as matzos, bread of affliction?

I would use a stringed instrument
to make jaguar sounds,
rattle in the long grass,

      tear open my poem's shirt, show
      bursting, purple and material,
      ringed with thorns
             the sacred heart.

Predicament

*Chronic pain is rampant, but there's no such thing
as chronic pleasure.*
—David Benatar, *The Human Predicament*

Seized in its lion paws, swallowed,
you'd faint from its jasmine breath
but it shakes you awake. Then, the colors.
You're a tuning fork set to every pitch.
Can't think of anything else. Can't
think. It'd leave you gasping, if
it would leave you. Try
to distract it so you can take
a little nourishment, sleep—
it roars back, savage joy.

Can you remember a time before
you were invaded, enveloped?
Remember the daily dark, old, dull,
when sidewalk puddles didn't bloom
with prismatic rings? Remember routines
of dress before your skin thrilled
to slippage and lacings? Take heart,
those days will come again, there's a cure
for chronic pleasure.

Lessons

If I don't sound exactly Bronx,
it may be because my mother
had me take elocution lessons.
All I remember is reciting
the tragic poem, "Casey at the Bat."

When I worked at Macy's
some people took me for English,
or anyway *not from here.*
The ballet lessons at 8,
meant to make me graceful,
not a success.

My mother had her small prides:
That she didn't take a chair
and sit in front of the apartment house,
that our four rooms were *off the foyer,*
that we lived *one flight up.*

In college I took Speech 1
and learned that when I said "bottle"
(bah-ul) I had a glottal stop.

Now I know that the Irishwomen
sat out on their kitchen chairs like cottagers,
the bar across the street was their pub,
where at night some sang
Peg O' My Heart with the men,
the glottal stop is the correct way
of saying ayin, the Hebrew letter
sometimes said to be silent.

I embrace the past with its shames,
its small differences,
my mother's ambition for me,
my neighbors' drunk nostalgia.

To reclaim the Bronx accent
with its sine-wave whine—
I think I won't.

My Desk Chair

Female, useful, you keep your dignity
though your lap's full of odd socks,
haphazard mending.

You were old sixty years ago,
dressed in Goodwill's sad maroon stain,
scarred with nailholes that once secured cane.

I stripped you, refreshed you
with paint the color of cantaloupe flesh,
and later with gay yellow.

Now dowager, throne, your sturdy arms
bear up my weight when my thighs sigh
and I need assistance to rise.

Patient, four-legged mount,
I think you will outlive me.
Last of a set of five, kept
when I let go of the side chairs,
I will leave you to heirs.

Unpacking My Books

Dust-catchers, tombstones,
You've fooled me
Into giving you breath and tears
When the stupidest cow has more life
Than you can claim.

What good are you in the dark
When I want to hear a voice, touch
A ribbed and breathing other?
What good are you, black and beige,
When I want scent and color?

You ask attention deserved
By plums and donkeys. You bricks,
If I could build a house with you
I would praise you.
Leaves, if I could eat you...

As it is, if I didn't fear fire
I'd take a match to you all.

Eighty

Age is just a number. —A liar

A number I boggle at, a hurdle. I've seen peers
like show-jumpers clear obstacles, ditches, drops;
some falter, fall. To me, 80 is a ha-ha, embedded wall
with a dry moat behind it—sneaky hazard, blind trap.

Madalon began to say *I'm in my ninth decade*
as soon as she turned 80. At 79 Sherry
declared herself 80 to claim the privileges
of help and courtesy. Nobody would think them
boring old aunts—Madalon stopped trying
to befriend golf players in her retirement village,
writes poetry, would still answer to *Tiger;*
Sherry smokes pot and paints abstractions.

Octogenarian sounds like a kind of dinosaur. Am I?
Careful not to type two spaces after a period, but
already I'm having trouble with technology, sigh
when the *New York Times* thinks to identify
the actress and model Marilyn Monroe.

Let me be a dinosaur—they get a bad rap.
They lasted longer than *Homo, habilis* and *sapiens*
put together. Call me a lumberer nibbling green things
or a glider with feathers, maybe red and green,
sibling to all those warbling two-leggers with wings.

I may meet the hurdle of 80 like Sherry,
at a canter, or like Madalon, galloping,
but let me not boggle at the obstacle;
horse people know that to boggle,
to lose confidence, is fatal. To fall.

While I Live

While I live, let me pour as through a sieve
the mixed and muddied waters of my loves,
hold the gold and let the silt go. While I live,
let me tilt the pan to the light, lift
ore from the stream, strain to haul nets
with gleaming gifts from the deep,
keep the good, leave the rest.

Grief hoards the gold and weeps
the human question, *Why not more,*
more life? For we hold our lost loves,
restored, only when we sleep.

Acknowledgments

I continue to be grateful to the people who encouraged me in poetry, especially Michael Wurster, Ellen Foos, the members of the U.S. 1 Poets' Cooperative, Pittsburgh Poetry Exchange, Squirrel Hill Poetry Workshop, Mike Schneider's East End Poets, and Madwomen in the Attic; and to my husband and my parents. Thank you to the editors who published the poems listed here.

B. Kissileff and E. Lidji (Eds.), *Bound in the Book of Life: Pittsburgh Writers Reflect on the Tree of Life Tragedy* (University of Pittsburgh Press, 2020): "Security Training — Stop the Bleed," "Tree of Life."

Eye Contact, Seton Hill University, (2016): "Unpacking My Books."

C. Gainey and E. Roussel (Eds.), *From the Ends of the Earth, Poems of the Eco-Justice for All! Inquiry.* (City of Asylum Pittsburgh Poet Laureate Program, Summer 2022): "Dear Editor:".

One Art (July 23, 2022)*:* "For Loneliness," "In the Night," "Mantis." https://oneartpoetry.com/

Paterson Literary Review, 50: "Lament for Cursive."

Pittsburgh Poetry Journal, 2: "Second Acts." http://pittsburghpoetry-journal.com/issue_2.html

PRISM: An Interdisciplinary Journal for Holocaust Educators, 14: "Yizkor (Remembrance Service)."

Daniel Weeks et al. (Eds.), *This Broken Shore* (Coleridge Institute Press, 2021): "Eighty."

U.S. 1 Worksheets: "Another Art," "My Desk Chair," "Security Training — Stop the Bleed."

Voices in the Attic (Carlow University): "By the Neva River, where I have never been" (in somewhat different form); "Resistance."

Vox Populi: "After the Emergence of the Periodical Cicadas," "The All-American Truck Stop," "Dead Russian Soldier," "More," "November," "Wordless." (voxpopulisphere.com)

Young Ravens Literary Review, 14 (Summer 2021)*:* "On the Land."

Arlene Weiner grew up in New York City. She lives in Pittsburgh, where she is active in Pittsburgh Poetry Exchange and the Squirrel Hill Poetry Workshop. She has been a Shakespeare scholar, a cardiology technician, a den mother, a member of a group developing educational software, and an editor. Her poems have appeared in a number of journals, including the *Paterson Literary Review, Pleiades, Poet Lore,* and *U.S. 1 Worksheets*; have been anthologized; and have been heard on *The Writer's Almanac*. Ragged Sky Press published two collections of her poems, *Escape Velocity* (2006) and *City Bird* (2016). Arlene was awarded a fellowship to the MacDowell Colony. She also writes plays. Pittsburgh Playwrights Theatre Company produced her play *Findings*, and Carlow University Theatre performed her monologue *Clothesline*.

www.ingramcontent.com/pod-product-compliance
Lightning Source LLC
Chambersburg PA
CBHW020214090426
42734CB00008B/1061